T0365610

As Wide As the Sky

by T D Biagas

illustrated by
Travis Thompson and Alex Thompson

Book Designer: Amuerfina B. Butron

To order additional copies of this book, contact:
Xlibris
844-714-8691
www.Xlibris.com
Orders@Xlibris.com

ISBN: Softcover 978-1-4134-9267-5
EBook 978-1-6641-9915-6

Library of Congress Control Number: 2005903238

Print information available on the last page

Rev. date: 11/11/2021

To my husband Kirt, and my sons, Chace and Dyson,
thank you for being my Joy and the reason I smile.

Love,
Me

Hi, my name is Chace,
and this is my brother Dyson.
Today, we are going to find out just
how much we are loved.

So, we are going to ask our
Mommy and Daddy.

"Mommy, " said Dyson.

"How much do you love me and Chace?"

"I love you both, **as tall as the mountain,"** Mommy replied.

Then Mommy raised her arms above her head to show us just how tall.

7

"Chace," said Dyson, "Will you show me a picture of a mountain?

I want to see how tall **a mountain** really is."

As, we were in our room
looking in our book at a mountain,
Daddy walked in.

"Hello, Boys," said Daddy, "what are
you guys doing?"

We are looking at a picture of a mountain.
Mommy said she loves us as tall
as a mountain.

"You, guys are so lucky,
because a mountain is really tall,"
Daddy said.

11

"Daddy, how much do you love us?"
asked Chace.

Daddy started looking through the book and he came across a picture that had water on it.

"Let me see, let me see," Dyson said with excitement, "I want to see!"

"You love us like water?" questioned Chace.

"Yes, I do but, this is a picture of the ocean," said Daddy. "I love you guys as long as the ocean."

"Whoa, that is a lot!" said Chace.

Daddy then stood up and held his arms up in front of him to show us how long.

We were so happy, because we knew just how much Mommy and Daddy loved us.

Before he left our room, Daddy, kissed us both and told us that he was so Glad That GOD chose him to be our father.

The next day, while we were at Church, Rev. Kimbrough told the congregation that **JESUS loved us so much that he died for us.**

Later that day, when we got home, we asked Mommy to show us a picture of

JESUS.

She showed us a picture of HIM on the cross. HE has HIS arms stretched out to the side.

"Look Chace look," Dyson said with extreme joy, **"JESUS loves us as wide as the sky."**

♫♪ ♫♪ I love you as tall as the mountain, as long as the ocean and as wide as the sky ... That's how much I love you ... That's how much I love you ... ♫♪ ♫♪

These two brothers want to know just
how much they are Loved,
so one day they ask their parents.
They soon find out who loves them
even more . . . . !

" I love you as tall as the mountain ,
as long as the ocean and as wide as the
sky, that's how much I love you . . . .
that's how much I love you . . . ."

T D Biagas came up with the song,
That's How Much I love You in 1997
when her first child was born. She later
put it in story form after having her
second child in 1999.

T D Biagas lives in Charlotte, NC with
her husband and their two sons.

Printed in the United States
by Baker & Taylor Publisher Services